D0913000

Lettering Simplified

Lettering Simplified

A manual for beginners by Rand Holub

Bonanza Books · New York

To my loving wife Helen

© MCMLVII *by* WATSON-GUPTILL PUBLICATIONS, INC.
All rights reserved • Printed in U.S.A.
Library of Congress Catalogue Card Number: 57-12739

This edition published by Bonanza Books,
a division of Crown Publishers, Inc.,
by arrangement with Watson-Guptill Publications, Inc.
a b c d e f g h

Contents

THE people of the United States are known far and wide for their manufacturing skills, their new developments in aviation and electronics, their time-savers on the farm and in the home, but I wonder if anyone has ever given us the title of "The Greatest Doodlers in the World?" Yet, glance at any telephone booth, subway poster or desk pad in a busy office, and you will see mustaches added to beautiful women, slogans changed on billboards, and grotesque specimens of handwriting, lettering, or just plain doodles.

With this thought in mind, and without expending much more energy, except for a little study and practice, I believe that the public can vastly improve their style and taste of lettering.

Naturally, there are other methods of approach to doing good lettering, but I think that the method which follows is practical and a start in the right direction. It may help the young student to do better posters, more legible signs, or start him on a career in the graphic arts.

Approach

As long as everybody loves to doodle, I know of no better method of loosening up your hand, and having fun with a pencil. Before you do, however, buy a fairly soft pencil, 2B-4B or 6B, and sharpen it to a chisel point like this —

or better still, buy a few of the sketching pencils that are oval and look like this  at the end. These are a little easier to use, and retain the chisel point naturally. Use a sanding block when the point becomes dull. Hold your pencil in this position and keep it at the same angle throughout.

Fill up a large page so —

If you keep the pencil in one position in your hand as you do this, you will notice a rather pleasing effect of thicks and thins. This pleasing effect is the basis for most of our well-designed type faces, lettering styles, border designs, and decoration. It is also the basis for many of the foreign language alphabets such as Arabic, Hebrew, Armenian, Greek, and others. Their form and character depend on the angle at which the letterer holds his chisel point.

Now do a little more doodling, but a bit more controlled this time.

Try some of these —

You will notice in these exercises that there is a definite design feeling, and if carried into your lettering, will improve it immensely

Basic Strokes
in the Capitals

THERE are not many basic strokes in the capitals of an upright alphabet, so now it would be a good idea to take a large sheet of paper and your chisel pencil (held in the position shown on Page 9) and fill up the page in this manner —

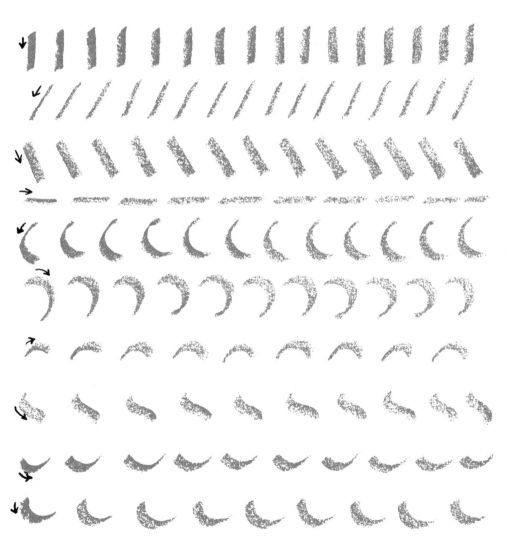

Arrows indicate the direction of the stroke

Construction
of the Capitals

*T*HESE are about all the strokes you need to draw the capitals, so let's start constructing the letters. Starting with the letter "A," as you draw your pencil down from top right to bottom left, you should get a fairly thin line. Now, joining at the top left and going diagonally to the right, your line is heavier — the width of your "chisel." Then about one-third of the way up you draw the horizontal, connecting the two diagonals, and that completes the letter.

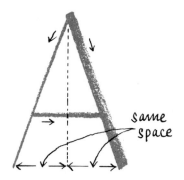

same space

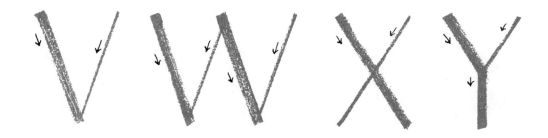

In all these letters, the important thing to remember is to try to keep the angle on the left the same as the angle on the right. Otherwise, you may get an effect of leaning backwards —

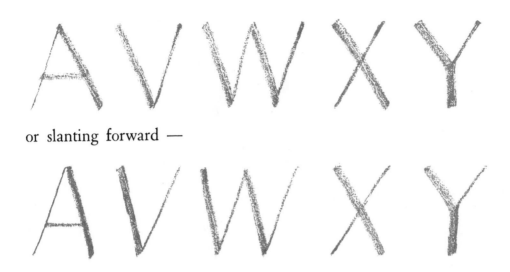

or slanting forward —

The letter "B," is a combination of a vertical stroke and two curves. Draw your vertical from top to bottom. Then draw the top loop a little above the center of the vertical. Connect the bottom loop and the "B" is finished. The top loop of the "B" is smaller than the bottom one.

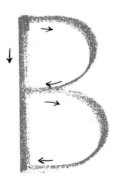

The same general construction applies to the letter "R." Keep the upright and top loop the same as in the letter "B." Then join the base of the loop with a diagonal running from left to right to the bottom of the letter.

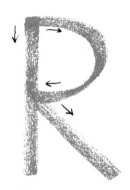

The "P" is constructed the same way, but with this difference, the loop is larger than that of the "R" and extends below the center of the vertical. This serves two purposes. It makes the letter more legible and, in lettering, there is less of a hole in the word.

Below center

The "D" is also in this family; however, in this letter the loop is the full size of the letter.

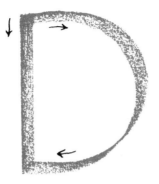

The next group of letters are mostly curved, so begin with the letter "O." Start the letter from the top, swinging leftward to the bottom. Then, in the next stroke, start at the top and swing to the bottom.

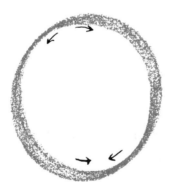

This is probably one of the most difficult letters to master, so don't be impatient or discouraged if the first few turn out badly. They will improve with practice. Remember to make these curved letters a little larger than straight letters, otherwise they will look smaller.

The "Q" is made in practically the same way as the "O," but a tail is added. This can be done in various ways — below are two examples.

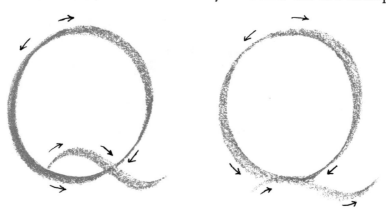

The "C" is also done the same way; however, after the left swing is completed, the right swing, starting at the top, goes only part way down.

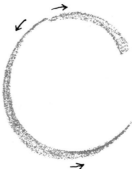

The "G" is drawn like the "C," but then a vertical and horizontal stroke are added — four strokes in all.

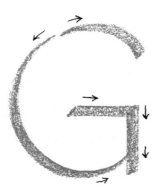

The letters "U" and "J" are in one group, so begin with the letter "U." Starting at the left top, draw your vertical and continue the line so that it curves over to the bottom right of the letter. Then draw your right-hand vertical to connect with this curve.

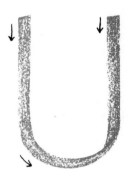

The letter "J" is constructed in an almost identical manner, but instead of starting the left downward stroke at the top of the letter it is started about two-thirds of the way down. Another way of making the "J," and probably a better one, is to begin with the right stroke, and finish with the loop at the left.

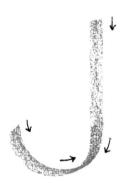

The letter "S" is a combination of three curves, and it can be done in either two or three strokes. To do it in two strokes, start at the top right and swing around so —

Finish the letter off by starting at the left and going around the bottom.

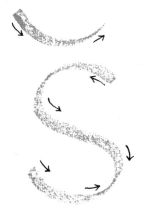

In the three-stroke method, start at the top left and swing right,

then connect at the left for the center curve,

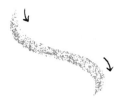

then finish off from left to right.

The second way, even though there is an added stroke, is easier to do and usually looks a lot better when finished.

The next group of letters that have much in common are the K, M, N, and Z. Begin the "K" with a vertical stroke, drawing from top to bottom. Then from the top right, draw a line diagonally to about the center of the vertical. Then, connecting at this point, draw the opposite diagonal, ending your stroke at the base directly under the start of the top stroke.

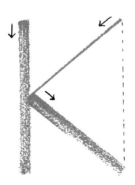

The "M" is a combination of two uprights and two diagonals. On the first vertical stroke, tilt the angle of the pencil so that your line is not as heavy as in a normal downward stroke. On the other three remaining strokes, however, return your pencil to the normal angle. When making the diagonals, try to keep the angle on the left the same as on the right.

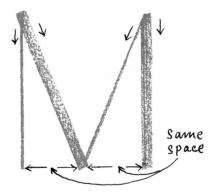

In the "N" as in the "M," the pencil is tilted to get a thinner vertical stroke. The diagonal is made with a normal stroke. In this letter, you may want to draw the two uprights first, and then the diagonal, or just follow in succession, upright, diagonal, upright.

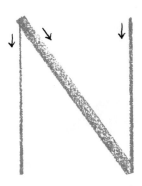

The "Z" is done in a normal position and starts with the top horizontal going from left to right. The diagonal is then drawn from right to left, connecting at the top. The bottom stroke is drawn from left to right. Bear in mind to keep the two horizontals the same length and directly under each other.

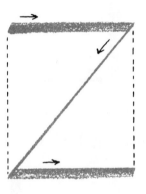

There are only a few letters remaining in the alphabet to consider, and these are composed of verticals and horizontals. They are the E, F, H, I, L, and T. As the "I" is the simplest, and also the basic stroke for all these letters, start with it, drawing from top to bottom. Its simplicity may fool you, so, before going to the other letters, do a line or two of "I"s, just as you did in the beginning of Basic Strokes.

The next letter that is closely related is the "L." Begin by doing the same downward stroke as in the "I," and then draw the horizontal from left to right.

The "H" is constructed by drawing the two verticals first, and then, a little above center, connecting these two with a horizontal.

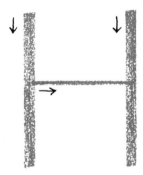

The "T" is made either by drawing your vertical first and then the top horizontal, or vice versa. No matter which method is used, make sure that the vertical is in the center, and that the two sides are even.

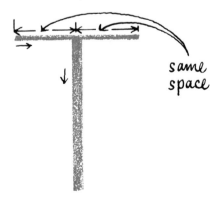

same
space

The "E," which is the most commonly used character in the alphabet, is started with the vertical stroke. The top and bottom horizontals are then drawn the same lengths, connecting to the upright. The center horizontal is drawn slightly above center, and extending not quite as far to the right as the top and bottom lines.

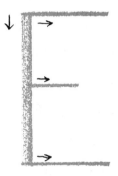

The "F" is constructed in almost the same way, but the middle stroke in this letter is dropped a little below center. As in the letter "P," this makes for better legibility, and also creates less of a hole in a word of lettering.

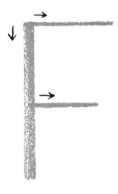

This completes the construction of the 26 capital letters and, for easy reference, the entire alphabet is printed on Page 31.

Construction
of Numerals and Symbols

BEFORE going into the construction of the lower-case letters, the numerals, symbols, and punctuation marks are such an important part of the language, that we will deal with them first. The basic strokes, except with slight variations, are practically the same. The student, by now, should have the feel of the pencil, and should have no trouble in making them. Numerals can be beautiful or ugly, depending upon the manner in which they are done.

The numeral "1" can be done in one stroke, but it is a little more graceful and more readable when started with a small loop, and then completed with a downward stroke.

The loop in the "2" is started on the left and swings to the right and down to the base of the number. The finishing horizontal stroke is then drawn from left to right.

The "3" can be made in two or in three strokes. To do it in two strokes, start at the top and swing to the right and down, keeping the loop a trifle above center. Then connect the bottom loop swinging in the same direction. The "3" done in three strokes is constructed in the same manner but the finishing stroke on the lower loop is drawn from left to right.

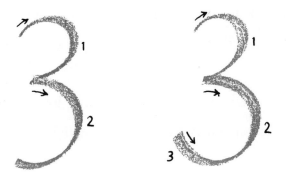

The "4" is started with a vertical, and then the diagonal is drawn starting from the top and drawing left about two-thirds down. The horizontal is connected to this, and drawn to the right, slightly passed the vertical.

The "5" should be done in four strokes to get the proper form. Draw the vertical and, as in the "M" and "N," tilt the pencil to keep the line thin. Attach the top horizontal going from left to right. Connect the loop to the vertical and swing to the right. The finishing stroke is from left to right.

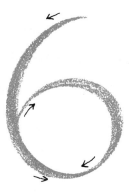

The "6" and "9" have a combination of small and large loops. These same loops are found in the letter "O," but there they are both the same size.

The "6" is started at the top with a large loop and swings to the left. The small loop starts midway and swings right, connecting at the bottom.

The "9" is started at the top with a small loop and swings to the left and under about halfway down. Then the large loop starts to the right and down.

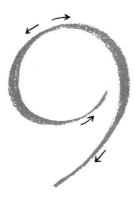

The "7" begins with the horizontal going from left to right. The diagonal then joins at the top right and is drawn to the base. This stroke should end a little to the right of the starting top stroke.

The "8" is started at the top and swings to the left, right, and down — in other words — an "S" curve. At the top draw the loop going right and down ending a little above center. At this point start the other loop going to the left and down, connecting with the "S" curve.

This numeral is a rather difficult one to master, so give it plenty of practice.

The exclamation point should be made in this manner. Start at the top and bring your pencil down. When you are part way down, release the pressure and thin out your line a little — then add the dot at the bottom.

The question mark is executed by starting at the top and swinging to the right and down, ending the stroke with a short vertical. The dot is then added.

The colon is made thus ⸬ and semicolon ⁏ a dash ⟶

Quotation marks are very frequently done wrong, but if the numbers "66" and "99" are remembered, they look like this " "

Parentheses are pairs of flattened-out loops, one starting from the top and swinging left and down; the other, starting at the top and swinging right and down.

In drawing the dollar sign, first draw the letter "S." Then add either one or two vertical strokes through the center of the "S," starting a little above and ending a little below. These lines should be kept thin by tilting your pencil slightly.

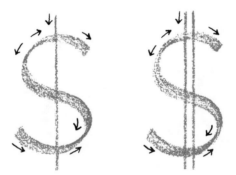

The cent sign can also be done two ways: Start by doing the letter "c." Draw the vertical through the center starting a little above and ending a little below the "c." The other way is to draw a short vertical above the "c," and another below.

Another important symbol that is used a great deal is the ampersand or "and" sign. Start at the top and swing left ending a little above center. Start the bottom loop at this point and swing left, around, and to the right. End with a short horizontal stroke.

And some variations

A B C D E

F G H I J

K L M N

O P Q R S

T U V W

X Y Z

Construction
of the Lower Case

$\mathcal{M}$ANY letters of the lower case are constructed the same as or similar to the capitals, so we will dispense with repeating them. These letters are the c, i, j, l, o, s, v, w, x, and z. The "i" and the "j" have a dot over them. The latter drops below the line. The basic strokes are also similar and have only a few variations. The size of the lower case as compared with the capitals is usually a little over one-half as large. A complete alphabet may be seen on Page 38.

The lower case "a" can be made in two ways, and both are acceptable. In the first case, draw a loop from the top and go left and down. Draw a vertical connecting the curve. The second one is started from the top and drawn to the right and then straight down. Draw the small loop starting a little above center, to the left and around.

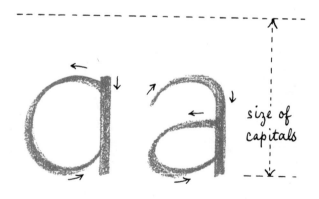

size of
capitals

The "d" is made the same as the first "a," except that the vertical or ascender extends above the line.

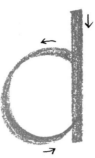

The "q" is also similar but the vertical or descender extends below the line.

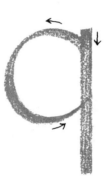

One form of "g" is also in this group. It is started like the first "a," but then the vertical is continued down and part way around. It is finished at the bottom with a left to right curve.

The other "g" is started like an "o." A small stroke is added to the top. At the bottom is added an "s" curve and the finishing curve is made from left to right.

The "b" and "p" are very much alike. In the "b," the vertical or ascender starts from the top (capital) line and is drawn to the base. The loop is then added swinging to the right.

In the "p" the vertical starts at top and descends below the line. The loop is the same.

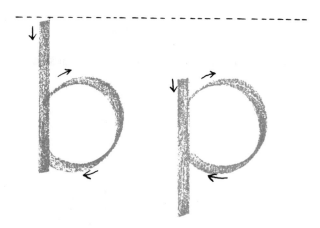

The "e" is constructed like the letter "c," but the right loop is brought down about half-way. The horizontal is then added from left to right.

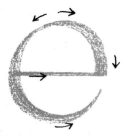

The "f" is begun from the top (capital) line with a short loop going from right to left and then down to the base with a vertical. A short horizontal is drawn across at the center line.

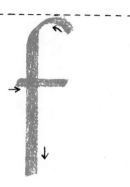

The h, m, n, and r are very similar in construction, and all start with a vertical.

The "h" starts from the top (capital) line, and a vertical is drawn to the base. A loop beginning a little below the center line curves up to the line and down.

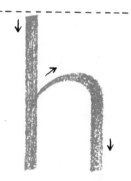

The "n" is made the same, but the first vertical starts at the center line.

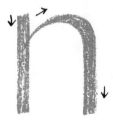

The "m" is not just an "n" with another loop added, but the loops are kept narrower, so that the letter does not become too wide.

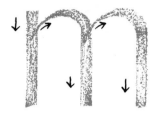

The "r" is constructed in much the same way. It begins with a vertical, but the loop is finished with a short stroke.

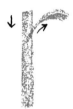

The "k" is done by drawing a vertical from the top (capital) line to the base. The top diagonal is drawn from the center line from right to left, and the lower one connects at this point and is drawn from left to right.

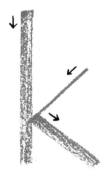

The "t" can be made in two ways. In the first, draw the vertical, starting a little above the center line, to the base. Then add a short bar at the center line. The second is started the same way, but before the vertical reaches the bottom a small curve is drawn.

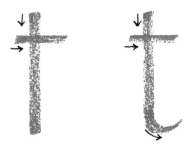

The "u" is made in two strokes. Starting at the left, a vertical is drawn down and then curved to the right. Another vertical is drawn connecting at the base to the curve.

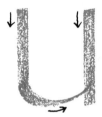

The "y" is started with the left diagonal and is drawn to the right to the base line. The right diagonal meets this line and extends part way down.

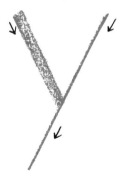

This completes the construction of the lower case letters and, due to the fact that some were omitted because of duplication, the entire alphabet is on the following page.

aabcd

efgghij

klmnop

qrsttu

vwxyz

Basic Strokes
in the Italic

As in the upright alphabet, take a large sheet of paper and a chisel pencil and try these strokes. With a fairly hard pencil, draw in the horizontals for the height of the letters. Then, very lightly, draw guide lines for the slant of the letters.

Construction
of the Italic Capitals

HESE guide lines will help train you in keeping the slope, curves, and angles more or less uniform. This slope can vary anywhere from 10 to 30 degrees, however, the greater the slope, the more difficult it is to keep the lettering legible. At the beginning, it is a good idea to keep the slope under 30 degrees. As in the upright alphabet, the angle of the chisel is rarely changed.

Italics come more naturally to most people as they usually write in a forward slant.

The italic "*A*" is constructed in the same manner as the upright "A." Here, again, it is important that the angle on the left be the same as on the right in relation to your slope line. It is started with the left diagonal at the top and is drawn left to the base. The right diagonal starts at the top and is drawn right to the base. The horizontal is drawn about one-third of the way up, connecting the two.

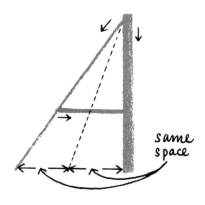

same
space

The other letters that follow this pattern are —

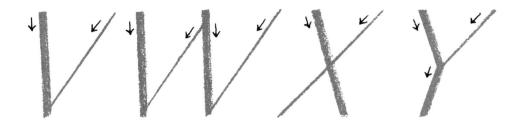

The *"B"* is made by starting with a downward stroke, following the slant you have set. The top curve is drawn from left to right and down, ending a little above center. The bottom curve connects to this and swings to the right and down. This curve is a little larger and wider than the top one.

The *"R"* is made in this manner, keeping the loop the same size as in the *"B."* The diagonal is drawn from left to right connecting at the end of the curve.

The *"P"* is executed similarly, except, as in the upright alphabet, the loop extends slightly below the center of the letter.

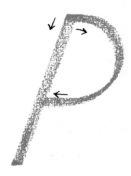

The *"D"* is started with a downward stroke, and then the loop is drawn the size of the letter.

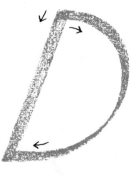

The *"O"* is started at the top, at the beginning of the axis. The first stroke swings to the left and bottom of the axis. The second stroke starts at the top and swings right to the bottom of the axis.

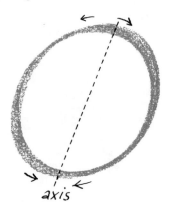

axis

Here, again, this letter should be done over and over until you feel that it is mastered. The same rule that applies to curved letters in the upright alphabet, also applies to the italic. Draw them a little above and a little below the line.

The "Q" is drawn as the "O," and then the tail is added. This tail can be done in many ways — below are three examples.

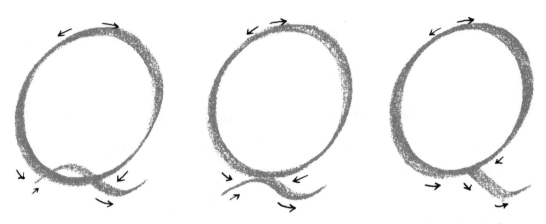

The method of making the "C" is similar to the "O," but the right stroke stops short and goes part way down.

The "G" is drawn in a like manner and, after the two curves are drawn, the short horizontal and downward strokes are added, finishing the letter.

The letter "U" is begun at the left with a downward stroke and continued in a curve to the right. The right-hand stroke is then made to complete it.

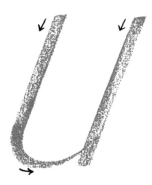

The "J" is started on the right with a downward stroke. The left stroke, starting about one-third of the way from the base, is then brought down and around.

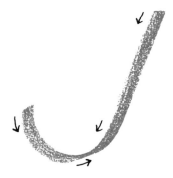

The letter "S" can be made in two or three strokes, just as in the upright alphabet on pages 18 and 19. In the italic, however, try to keep the curves and form of the letter by following the correct slope. The upper part of the "S" should be slightly smaller than the lower. As in the letters "O, Q, C, G" and other curved letters, draw the letter a little above and below the line.

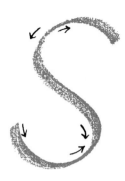

The *"K"* is begun with a downward stroke. Then, from the right, a diagonal is drawn to about the center of the stroke. Connecting at this point, the lower diagonal is drawn to the base.

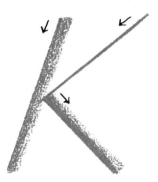

The *"M"* is started on the left with a downward stroke, tilting the pencil to get a thin line. Draw the right downward stroke, returning the pencil to the normal angle. From the top left, draw a diagonal to the center, and from the top right draw a diagonal to the center.

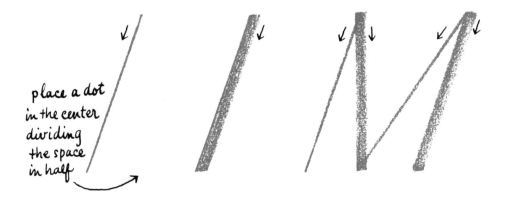

place a dot
in the center
dividing
the space
in half

The pencil is tilted in the two downward strokes of the *"N."* The diagonal is drawn with a normal stroke.

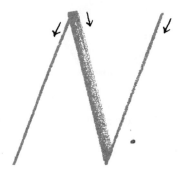

The *"Z"* is begun at the top left and a horizontal is drawn to the right. The diagonal starts at this point and is brought down to the left. The finishing stroke is drawn to the right. Line up the top and bottom strokes.

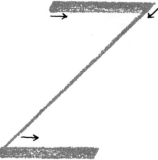

The *"I"* is simply a stroke going from top to bottom.

The *"L"* is a combination of this stroke with the addition of a horizontal stroke at the base.

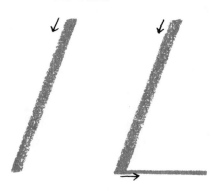

The *"H"* is made by drawing two downward strokes, and then connecting them with a horizontal a little above center.

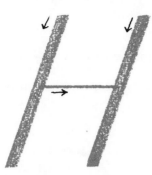

The *"T"* is begun with a horizontal and then, at the center, a downward stroke completes the letter.

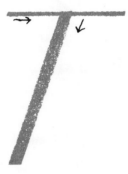

The *"E"* is drawn starting with the downward stroke. The top and bottom horizontals are drawn, and then, a little above center, the middle stroke is made, slightly shorter.

The *"F"* is done in this manner, but the second stroke drops a little below center.

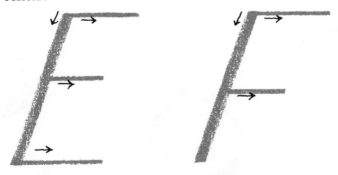

This completes the construction of the 26 italic capital letters, and the entire alphabet is on page 50.

Construction
of Italic Numerals and Symbols

Without further ado, and with only the arrows to point the direction of the strokes, here are the numerals and symbols of the italic alphabet.

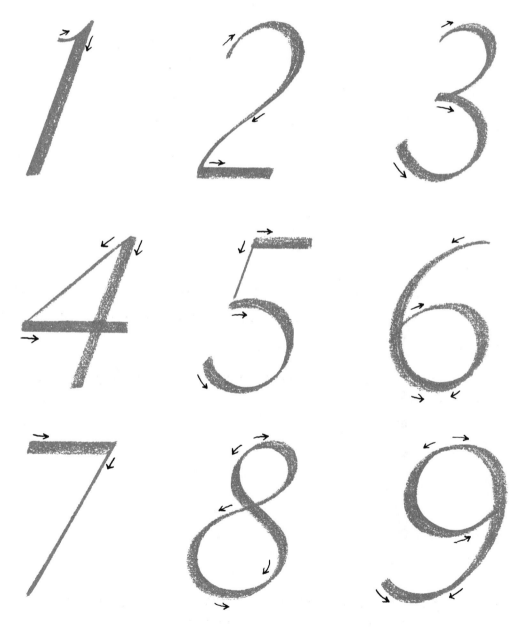

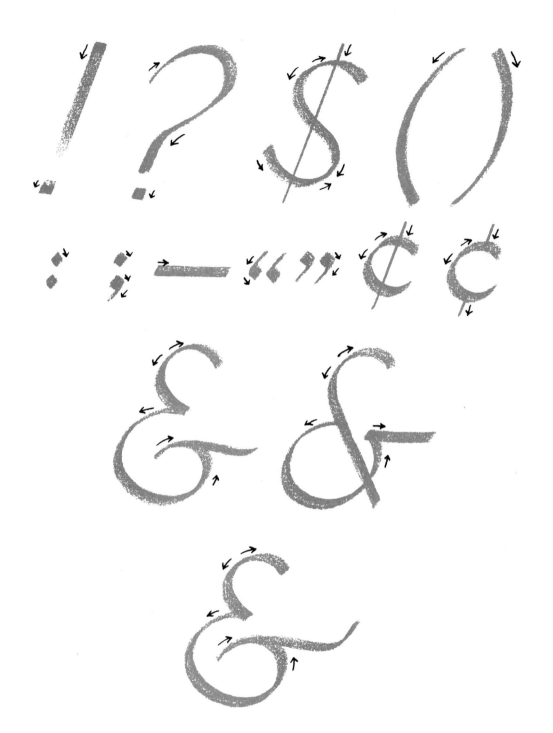

A B C D E
F G H I J
K L M N
O P Q R S
T U V W
X Y Z

A s in the upright lower-case letters, there is a great deal of repetition in construction in the lower-case italics. Many of these letters will be omitted, but a complete alphabet is on Page 56.

The italic lower case *"a"* can be drawn in two ways. In the first, start a loop from the top and go left and down. Draw a straight line, following the guide line for the proper angle, connecting the curve. In the second "a," start at the top and go right and down. The small loop starts a little above center and goes left and around.

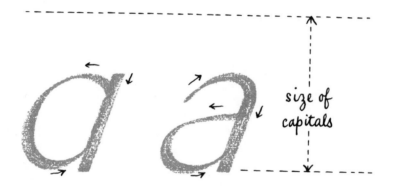

size of capitals

The *"d"* is drawn as the first *"a,"* but the ascender extends almost to the capital line.

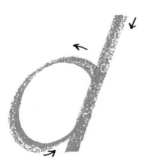

The "*q*" is also made this way, but the descender extends below the line.

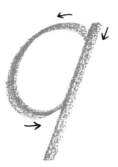

The "*g*" is executed in a like manner, with the addition of a small loop at the bottom, which goes from right to left.

The "*b*" is started from the top (capital) line and is drawn to the base. The loop connects to this and swings right and down to the base.

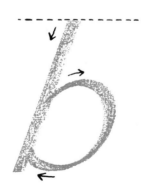

The "*p*" starts from the top and extends below the line. The loop is the same as in the "*b*."

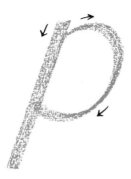

The "*e*" begins at the top and swings left and around. The other curve starts from the top and swings right about half way down. The horizontal connects these two curves.

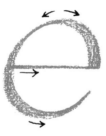

The "*f*" starts from the top (capital) line with a short loop and then continues down to the base. A short horizontal completes the letter.

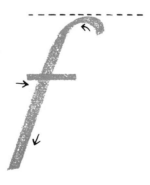

The "*h*" starts from the top (capital) line and is drawn to the base. The loop starts a little below center, curves up to the center line and down.

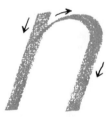

The "*r*" is similar, but the first stroke starts at the center line and the loop stops short.

The "*n*" starts like the "*r,*" but the loop continues as in the "*h.*"

The "*m*" is constructed as the "*n,*" but the loops are a little smaller and closer together.

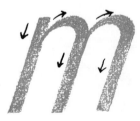

The "k" starts from the top (capital) line and is drawn down. The top diagonal goes from right to left, and the lower one, connecting at this point, from left to right.

The "t" starts a little above center and is drawn to the base. A short horizontal finishes the letter.

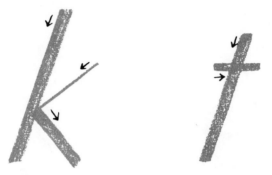

The "u" begins with a down stroke and continues around and over to the right. Another down stroke completes it.

The "y" is constructed starting with the diagonal drawn left to the base. The right diagonal is then drawn and extends part way down.

*The complete italic lower-case alphabet
is on the following page.*

abcde
fghijk
lmnop
qrstuv
wxyz

*N*ow that you have practiced the various alphabets, the next step is putting them into words and sentences. This requires not only good form in letters but also good spacing. The term *good spacing* does not mean taking a ruler and measuring off an equal distance between letters. This will result in very poor spacing —

MATERIAL

This word was measured off with a ruler and, as you can see, results in a word that is not pleasing because the "color" or tone is not uniform. Here's what happens when the word is spaced out without measuring, adjusting letters according to their weights and white space surrounding each individual letter.

MATERIAL

Mechanical aids such as a T square and triangle are fine for drawing guide lines for the height or slant of the letters, but do not allow these instruments to become your master. There is nothing to take the place of an artist's eye when it comes to spacing out a word or line of lettering. There are some general rules about spacing that are important to remember.

When two straight letters come together such as "MI," a little more space should be left between them, otherwise an optical illusion is formed by the parallel lines which makes them seem closer than they actually are. This applies whether you are doing the upright letters or italics.

If a straight and a curved letter are adjacent, such as "MO," they can be a little closer, because of the white space surrounding the "O."

When two curved letters come together, such as "CO," they can be even closer.

The "LA" combination, (such as in the word APPLAUSE), is a difficult one, and unless the horizontal stroke on the "L" is shortened, or if the line of lettering is letter-spaced, there will be quite a hole in the word.

The term *letter-spaced* means that there is more than the usual amount of space between letters. If a line of lettering is done this way, then a proportionate amount of space must be left between words. If this is not done, then the entire line will tend to run together, and be illegible. In ordinary spacing, too, leave enough space between words so that they are easily read. The other extreme is leaving too much space between words. This results in a very jumpy line and, instead of reading it as a sentence, it is read as separate words. There is no set rule as to how far words should be spaced apart, but it is up to the artist's good judgment to design a beautiful, pleasing, and legible line of lettering.

NORMAL
SPACING

L E T T E R
S P A C I N G

Normal
Spacing

Serifs

*T*HESE strokes, that are used in some alphabets to terminate letters, help to give a certain character that identifies that particular style of lettering or type face from another. In many instances, they also make for better legibility. The shapes, sizes, and ways of doing them are as varied and unlimited as the artist's imagination.

Through the ages, many styles of serifs have been used, some good and some bad. In many cases, the flavor of a certain period in history can be duplicated by following the style that was in vogue in that era.

To best illustrate some of the varieties of serifs, below and on the opposite page are some examples of type faces. The form, weight, and proportion are different in each, yet the serif plays an important part in determining the type face.

B A B C D E F G H I J K L M N O P Q R S T U V W X Y Z
odoni

C A B C D E F G H I J K L M N O P Q R S T U V W X Y Z
aslon

G
ABCDEFGHIJKLMNOPQRSTUVWXYZ

Garamond

S
ABCDEFGHIJKLMNOPQRSTUVWXYZ

Stymie

C
ABCDEFGHIJKLMNOPQRSTUVWXYZ

Century

L
ABCDEFGHIJKLMNOPQRSTUVWXYZ

Latin

V
ABCDEFGHIJKLMNOPQRSTUVWXYZ

Verona

For complete fonts of these and other type faces, there are many books at the Public Library, art supply store, or they usually can be gotten from type foundries or type setters. These contain the capitals, lower case, and italics in the many weights and sizes. Try drawing them all to get variety into your work.

Remarks

*I*F you have come this far, and found that lettering is not boring, but seems to grow on you more and more, you will not be satisfied with the few simple alphabets that are in this book. You will start to acquire other books with more advanced styles, or go to the Public Library and borrow books so that you may practice in your leisure time. Many of the old manuscripts have classic examples rendered by master penmen.

At times, too, disregard your T square and triangle completely, and just letter words and sentences on a sheet of paper and, afterwards, see how straight you've kept them. This is good training, especially when you are doing rough layouts, whether for advertising, posters, book jackets, or signs.

Try doing some of the sans serif (without serifs) type faces such as Futura, Franklin Gothic, Venus, and Neuland, and see how interesting they are.

Clip out pages of lettering in magazines or newspapers that you like, and try drawing them.

Try to obtain specimen sheets of type faces from the many type foundries and practice with them. Many people do not realize that such classic type faces as Caslon, Bodoni, Baskerville, and others were named after men who designed them. They were actually hand-lettered alphabets that were later cast in metal.

And finally, when your hand and wrist get a little tired, loosen up and try some of this for fun.

The End